AF479841

VITAE

VITAE

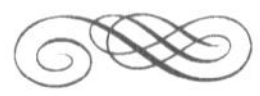

*A collection of poems
and photography*

MIRANDA SANTORO

Miranda Santoro

To my 7th grade English teacher, who always said I'd one day write a book. And to my cat Binx, who persistently tried to add his own poems by walking across the keyboard incessantly. Sorry they didn't make the cut, little gremlin.

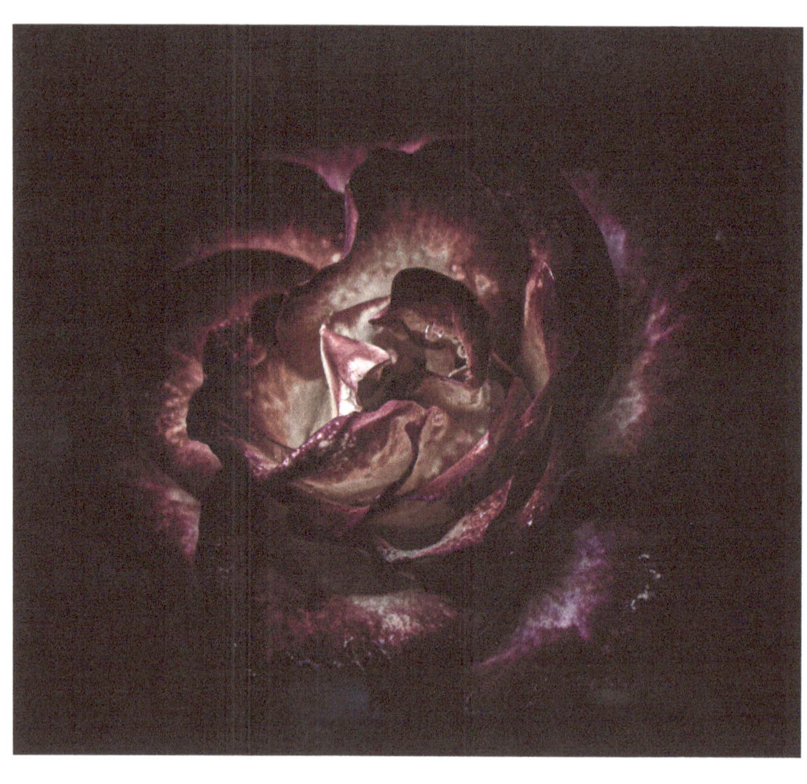

BLACK

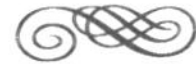

Lost souls
Drink ink.
But only wither,
With the weather.
Like roses,
Red-
And dead.
But they're beautiful,
You know.

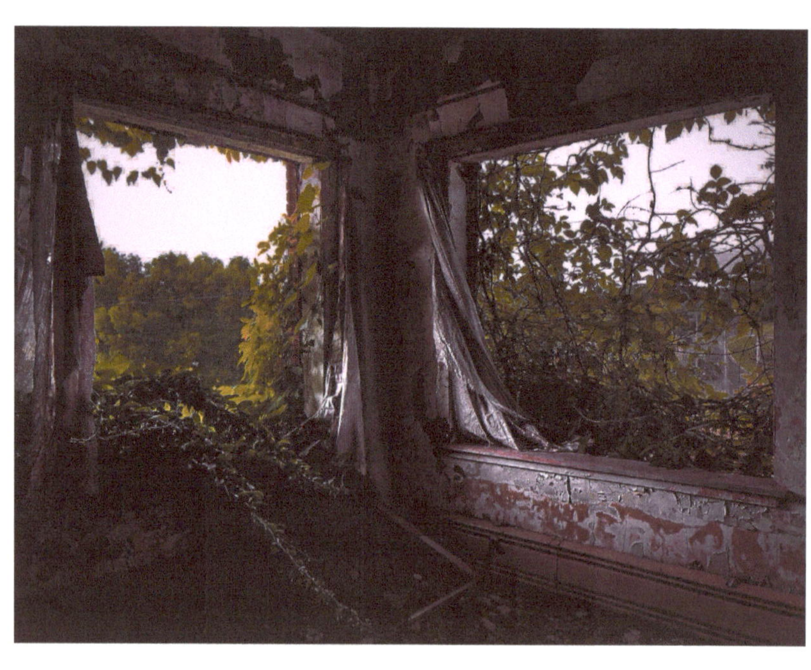

A NEW PLACE

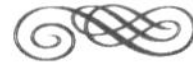

A listless ghost sits
On an empty shelf. She
Sees a universe in the dust
Speckled on forgotten wood.
The memories are small -
Perhaps even lost - but with
Time and space they grow
Infinitely within the dark,
Until one night they illuminate
A sky so vast and bright
Our listless ghost can't help
But to marvel at the sight.

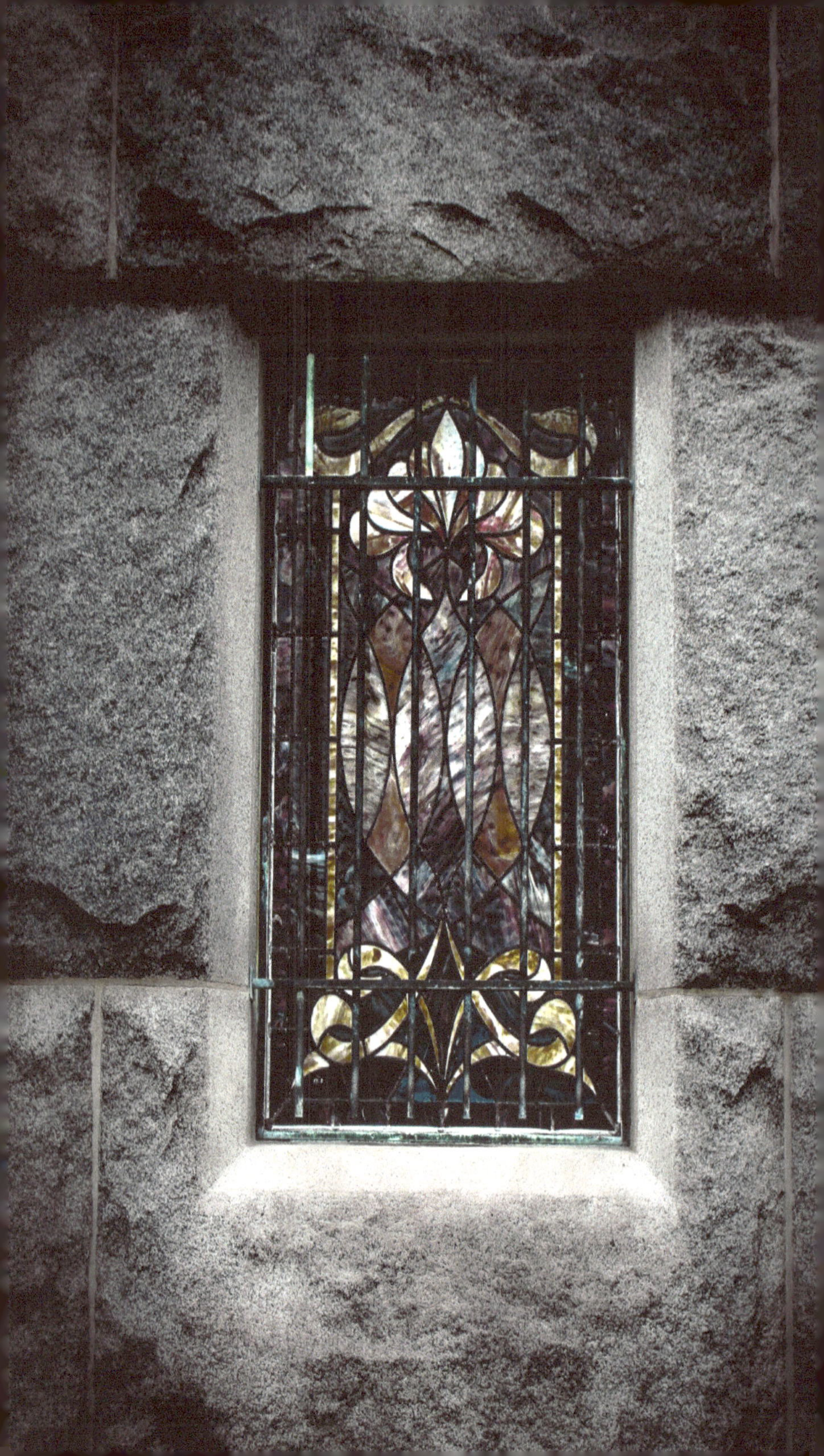

OTHER WORLD

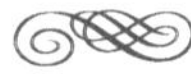

Take this window for example;
These words a world to some unknown,
Where untold stories will always roam.
For here, Creation and her cosmic song
Play sweetly along a love of Destruction.
See, one cannot exist without the other -
A question of contrast to discover -
Birth & death, with everything in between,
What is light without shadow?
Reality without dreams?

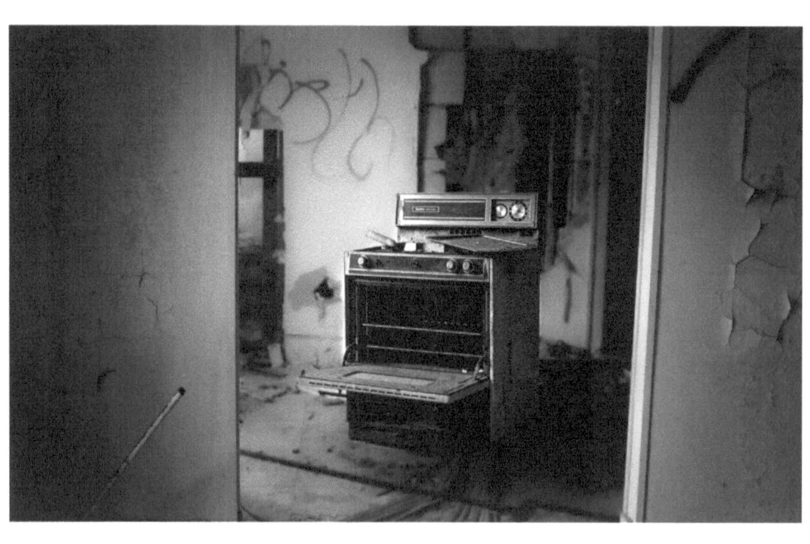

REMEMBER?

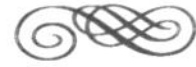

The color of memory
Sings a strange tune -
Time strums its' strings
So from it fades nothing
To anew.
And so,
I am a chameleon of chaos -
A kaleidoscope of the senses;
Time accompanies with a cacophony
Of a storm which coalesces.

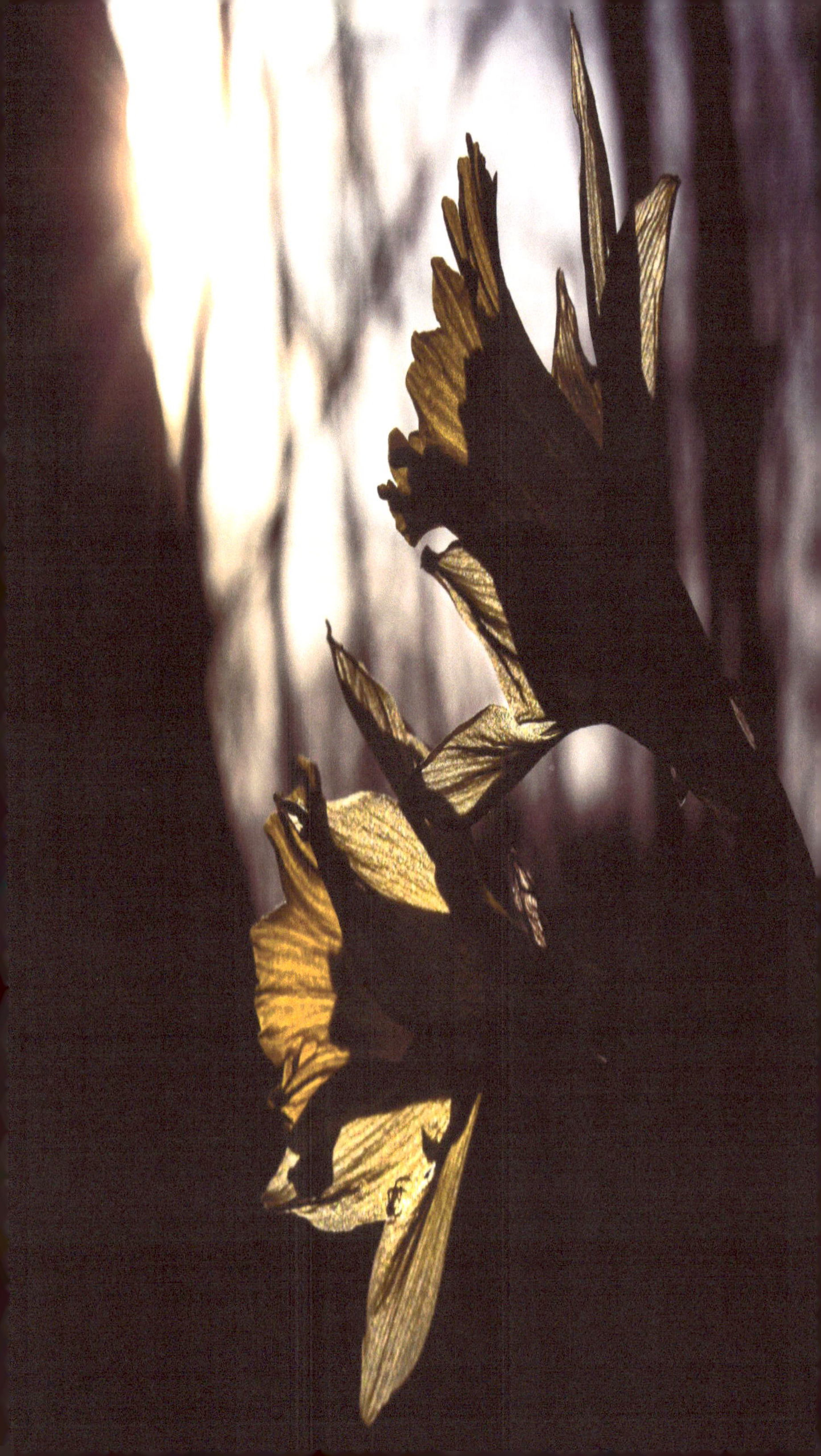

DANCING WITH SHADOWS

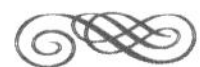

Let us walk amongst this chaos,
My friends. The demon inside us
Knows how to dance. And why not?
Take the bloodstained hand and
Bring warmth to the flesh so hell
Bent on death? Does this sinister
Figure not look familiar? I think
You have seen them. Been intimate;
So what's left but to waltz with
Our shadows? These scars a
Score etched onto our skin - such
Sweet crescendo until Death's end.

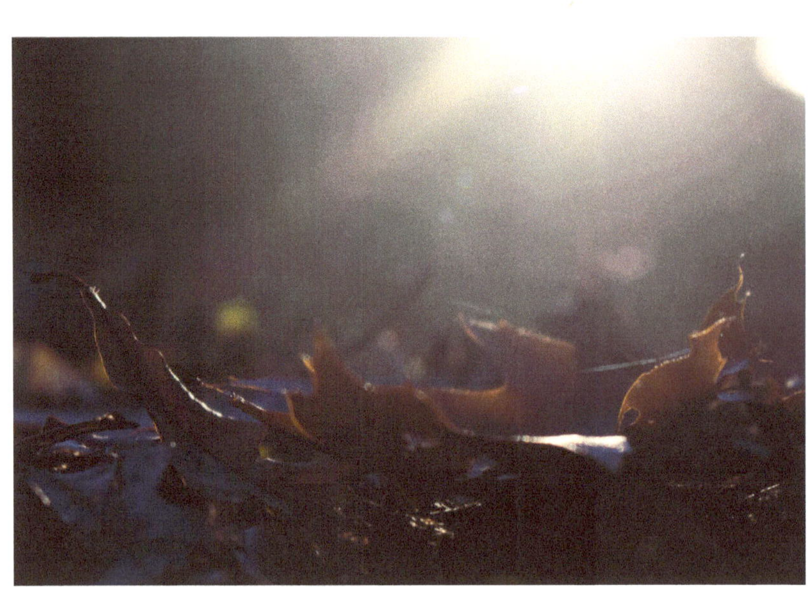

And Then Fall

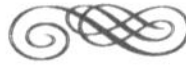

And now death -
This haunted end nears -
For all leaves lament

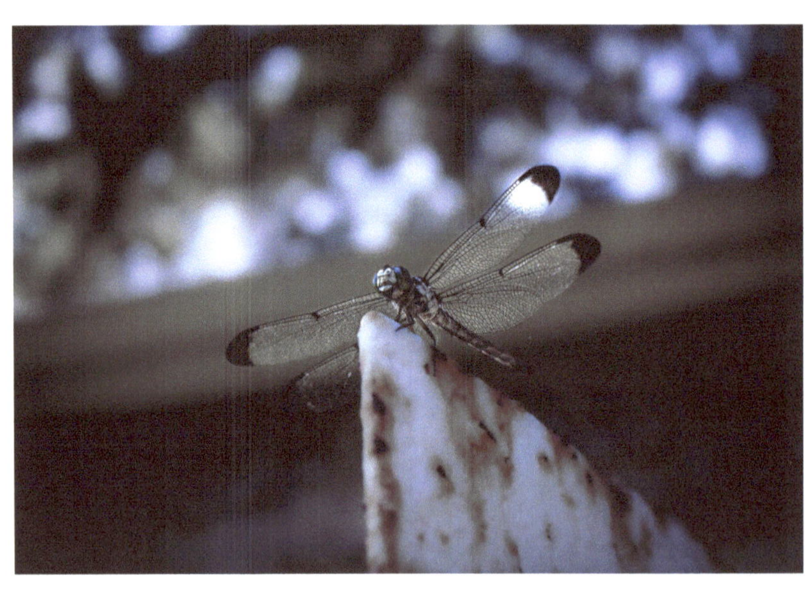

THE DRAGONFLY KING

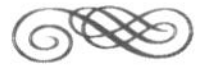

Do not vex our
King of the wind - for
Those of star-crossed fate
Will weep at his feet. See,
Mercy is not meant for
Ill-begotten minds - sickened;
Void of selflessness or virtue -
Fine character of any kind.
Forever, it seems, they sleep;
Condemned to bed their ignorance -
One does not grow without consequence.
So no, mercy is not for the
Malnourished self. Disappointment
In death is what is to be felt. This
Is the punishment of our King -
Grieve, little souls, for all of your kin.

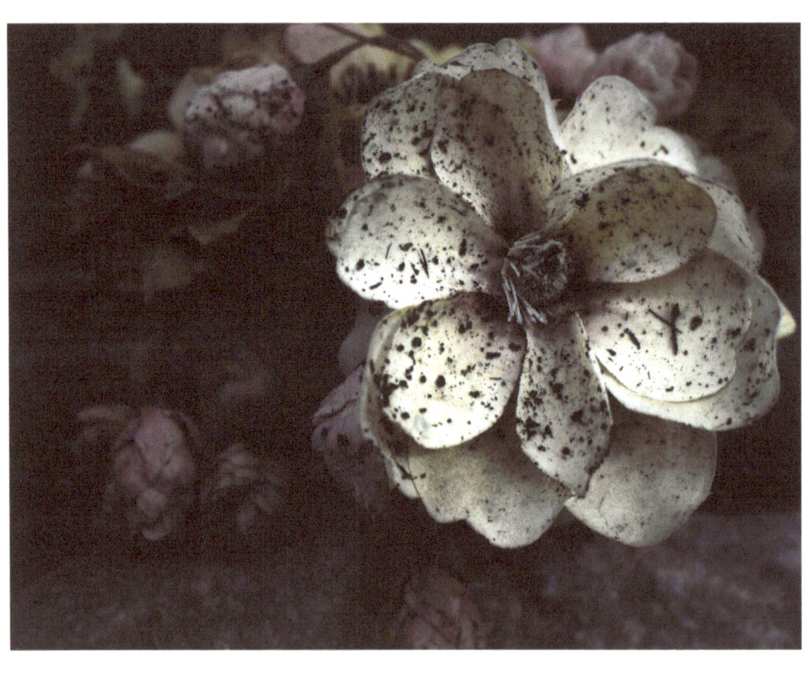

DEATH OF FIREFLIES

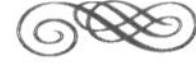

We are the children that
Dissect delicate bodies in the
Hopes of owning their light. So
I suppose it's no surprise that
The blood of penniless people
Gives life to gardens of elite, and
Feeds the gruesome fruit they eat.

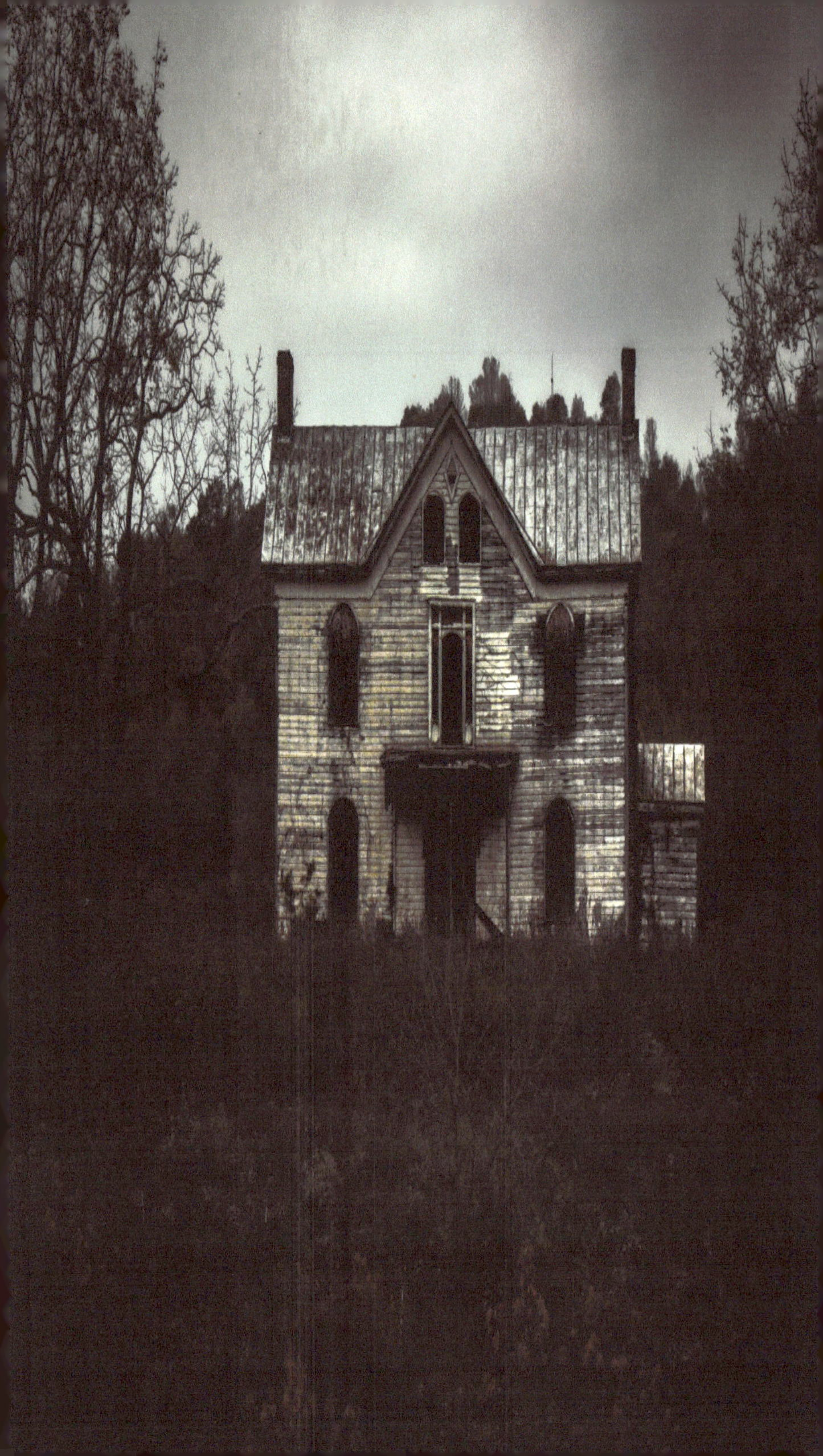

Black, Pt. 2

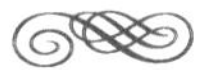

-Remember each death-
I'm a broken record, replaying -
-And never deem days eternal as death-
Words like my teeth are rusted,
Red from the iron in my blood.

-And never deem-
Motor locomotive, spewing
-Days eternal as death-
Old words,
My mouth black with exhaust.
-But it's beautiful-
I am rusted
-You know-

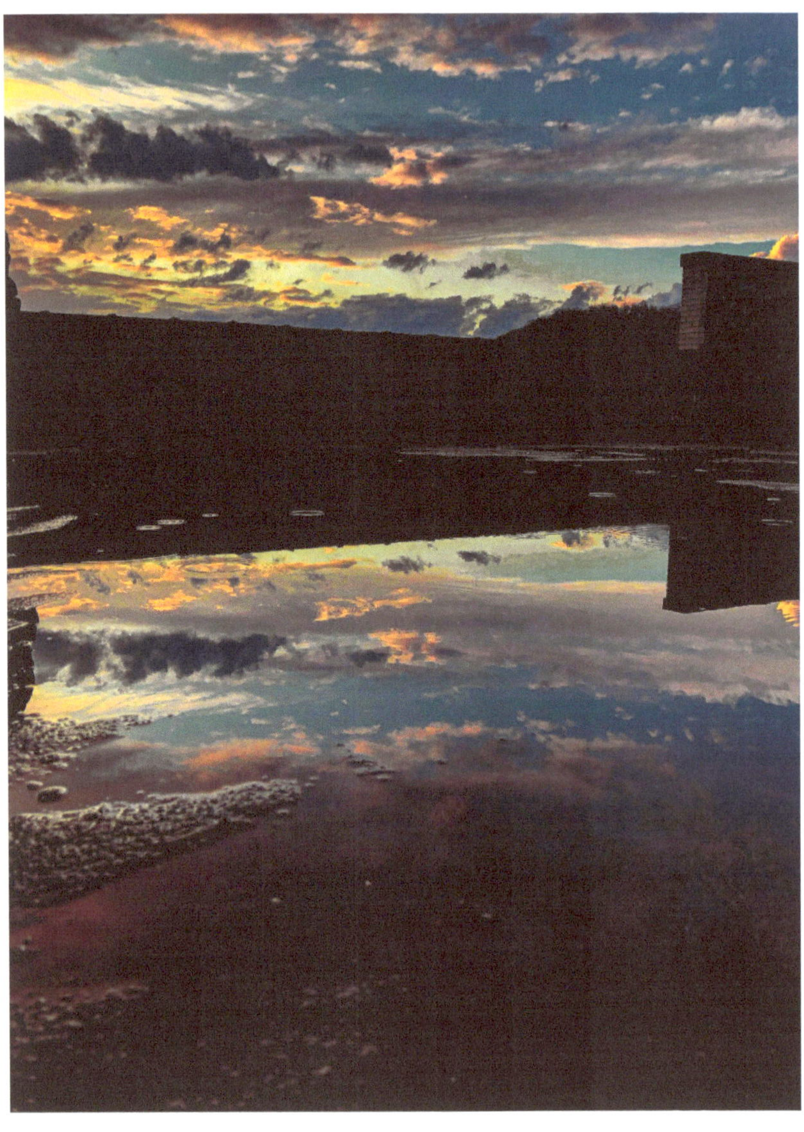

See Both Worlds

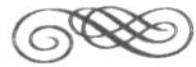

Such enigmatic eyes,
Beautiful on the horizon.
Where often rebirth lies, distant skies.

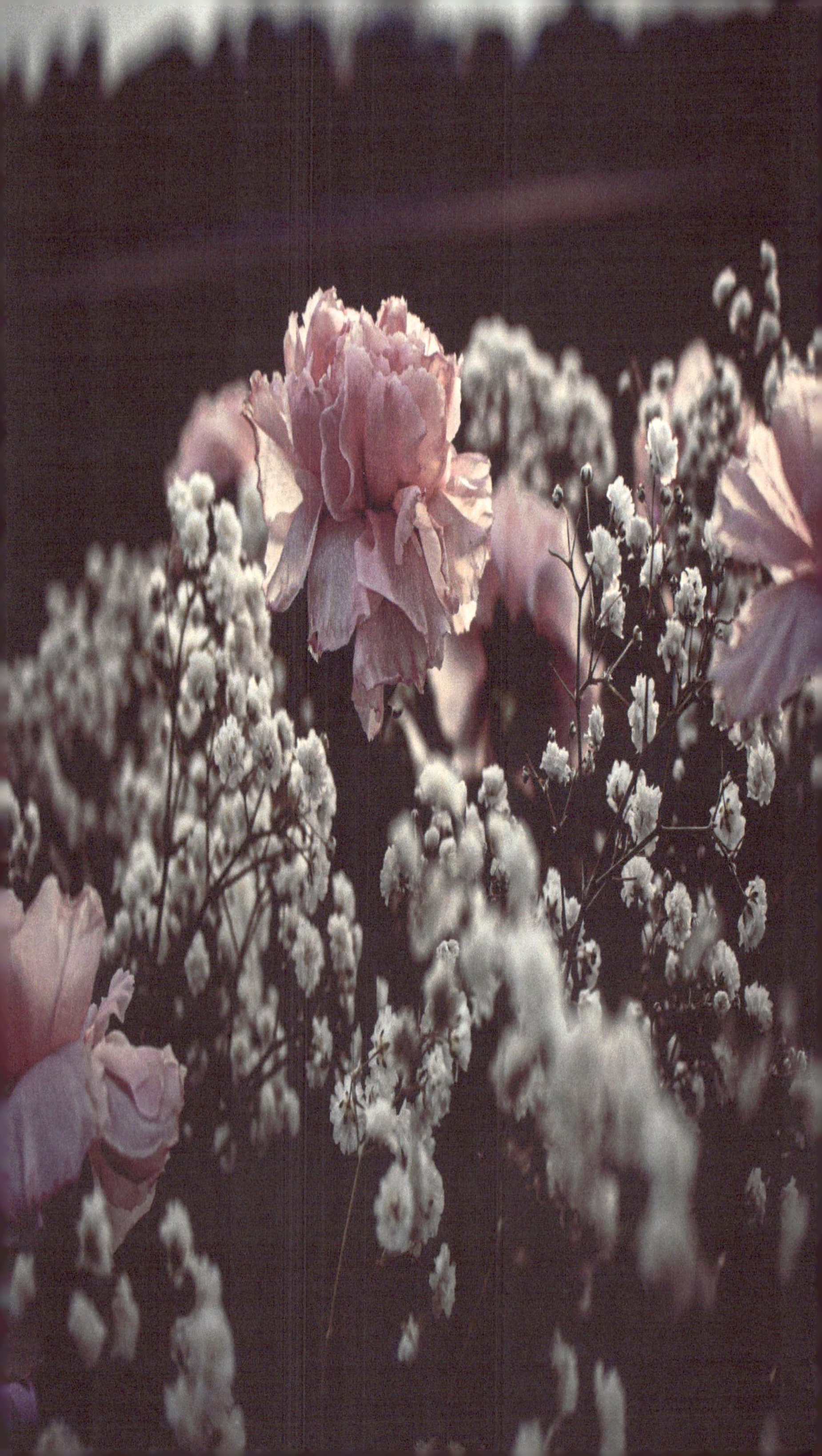

To Breathe Easy

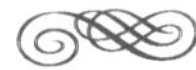

This one
Beautiful ride ends - and though hell, every
Essential adventure saves you.

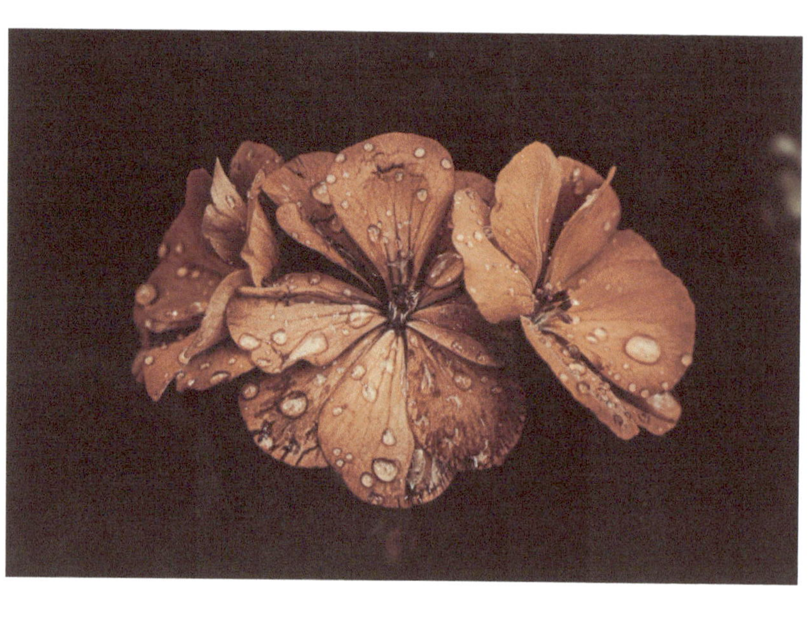

THE VEINS OF NIGHT

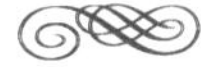

It's the first night with windows open;
Small taps of water on pavement keep time
With wind humming through leaves -
The earth breathes and sighs in its sleep.
Moments seem to last forever - as if
Ethereal flowers drip eternities into
Puddles at my feet. The future and past
Pool around my toes - eons spill into
Crevices and cracks in the ground.
All while quietly still - the rain drops
And drowns every sound into hushed
Tones as it drums to the beat of life; or
The beat of blood rushing through veins
In stillness as we sleep.

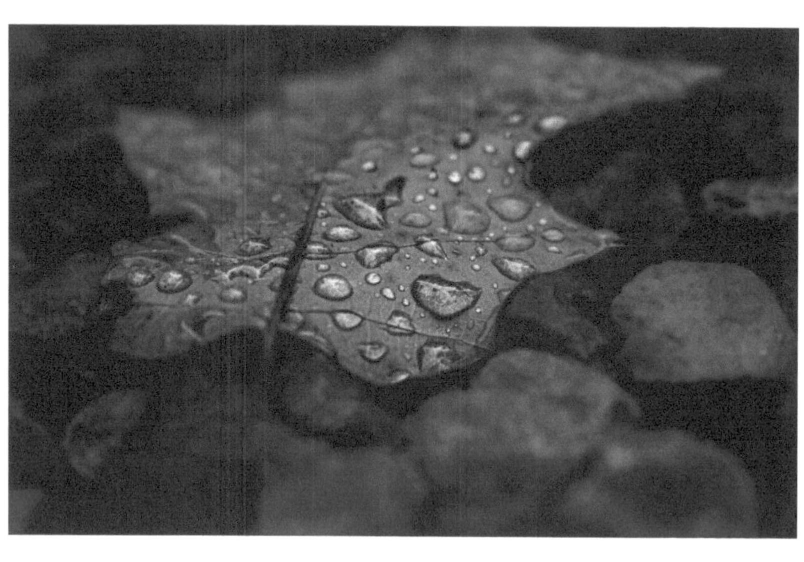

DROPS OF RAIN

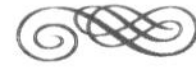

Tucked amongst forgotten rubble,
A thousand eyes reflect my wonder.
Such small worlds within the water
Wait amidst their wistful brethren -
So at odds with my own perception.
For they are tiny and I am large -
Yet, perhaps relation is not so far
And I, too, am a raindrop in a storm,
Only stars drip while wind roars
And the universe is a tempest to explore.

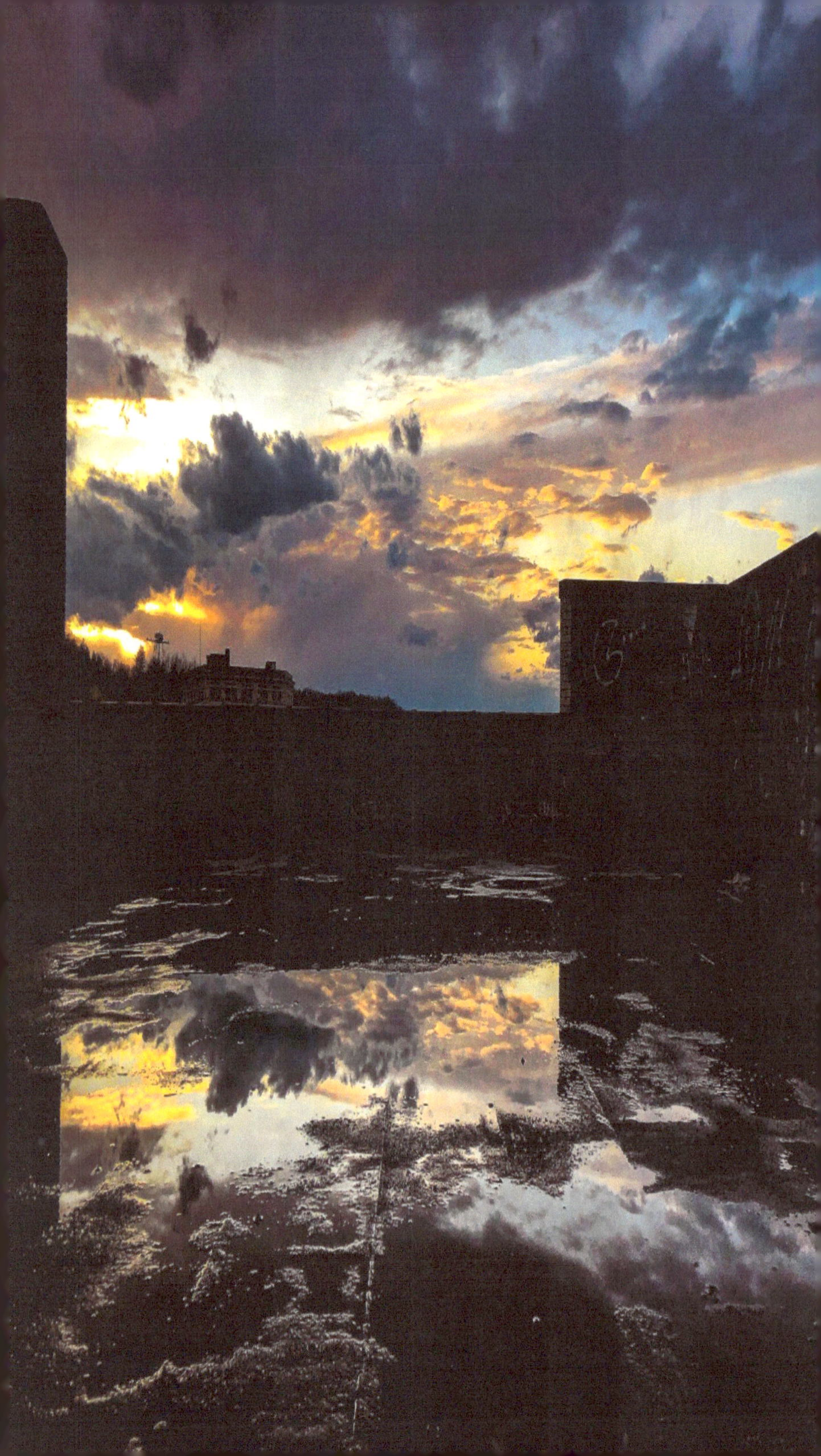

EARTH

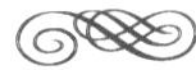

Galaxy of blue and purple,
I trace the reflection of stars
With fingertips dewy in birth
And death on my breath;
Tsunami of a butterfly is
The wind at my lips, I kiss
The clouds that confined me.

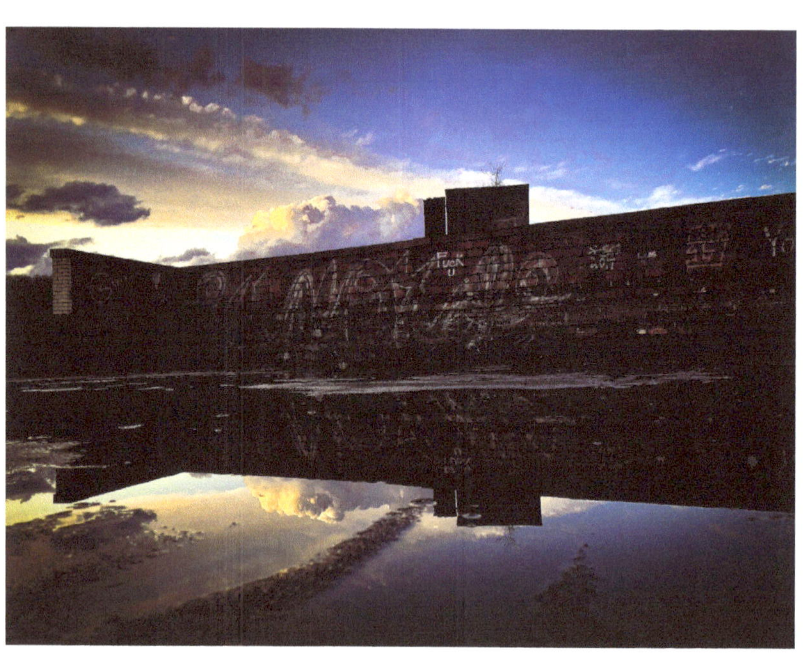

REFLECTIONS

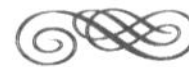

I watch the clouds slip past
In the reflections they cast;
The scattered about puddles
Stretch for miles and miles.
And aren't we all? Reflections
Of the experiences we bear;
All scattered about time,
And stretching across years.

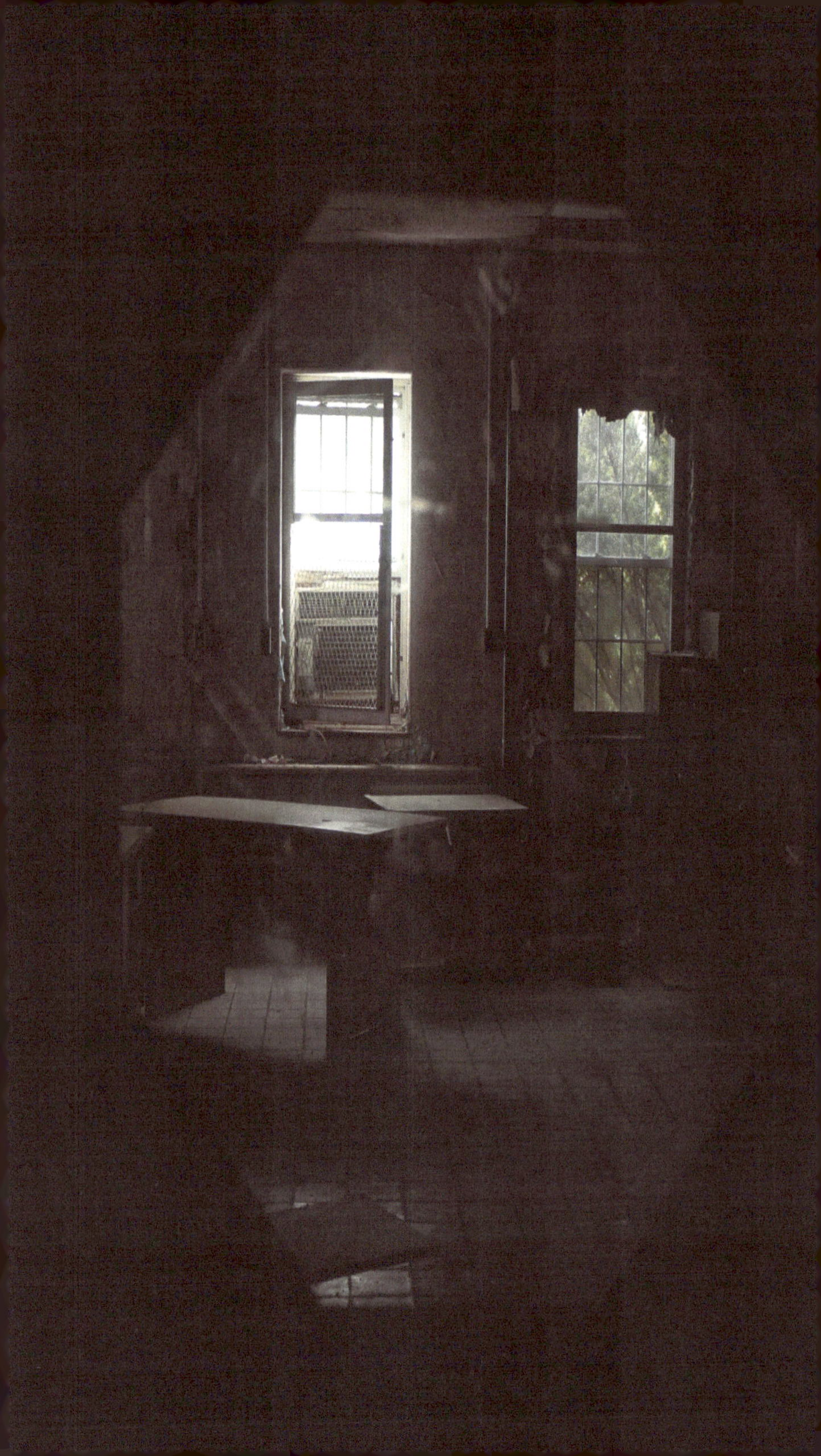

EFFERVESCE

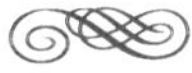

Today I saw a tiny bubble
Dodging damp bullets between
Dirty sidewalks and blackened drains -
The rain of colors swirled in a world
Inverted, and my renege sister stared;
Caged, as she was, by such fragile walls of air.

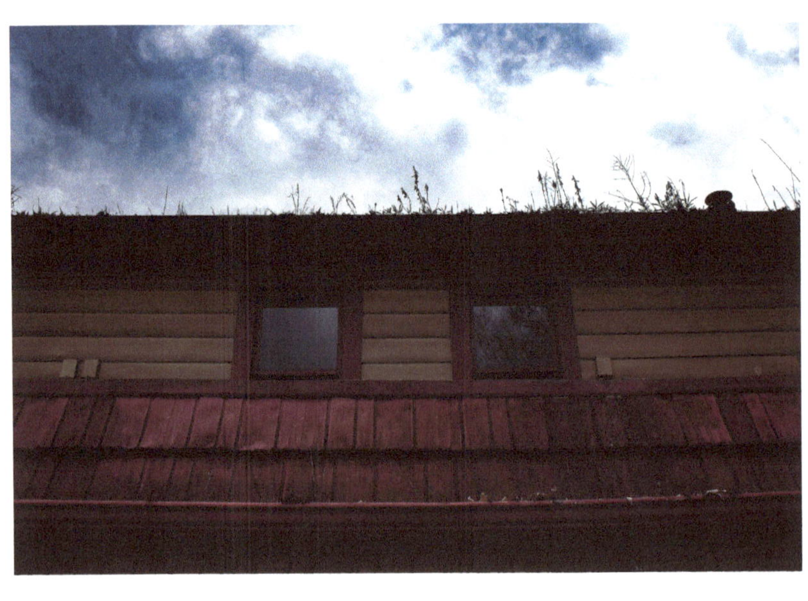

URBAN WALLFLOWER

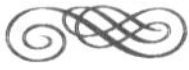

A lonely girl fell in love
With the city skylines in
The horizon of time and
Distance. She lived for
Taking walks & watching,
Listening, being near all
The different stories who
Talked like she couldn't;
She had never learned to.

Her solitary soul found
Peace in pacing streets;
In passing and passively
Partaking in this company.
Perhaps a small smile or
A windswept "hello", she
Was happy. Always near
But never with, just this.
She needed nothing more.

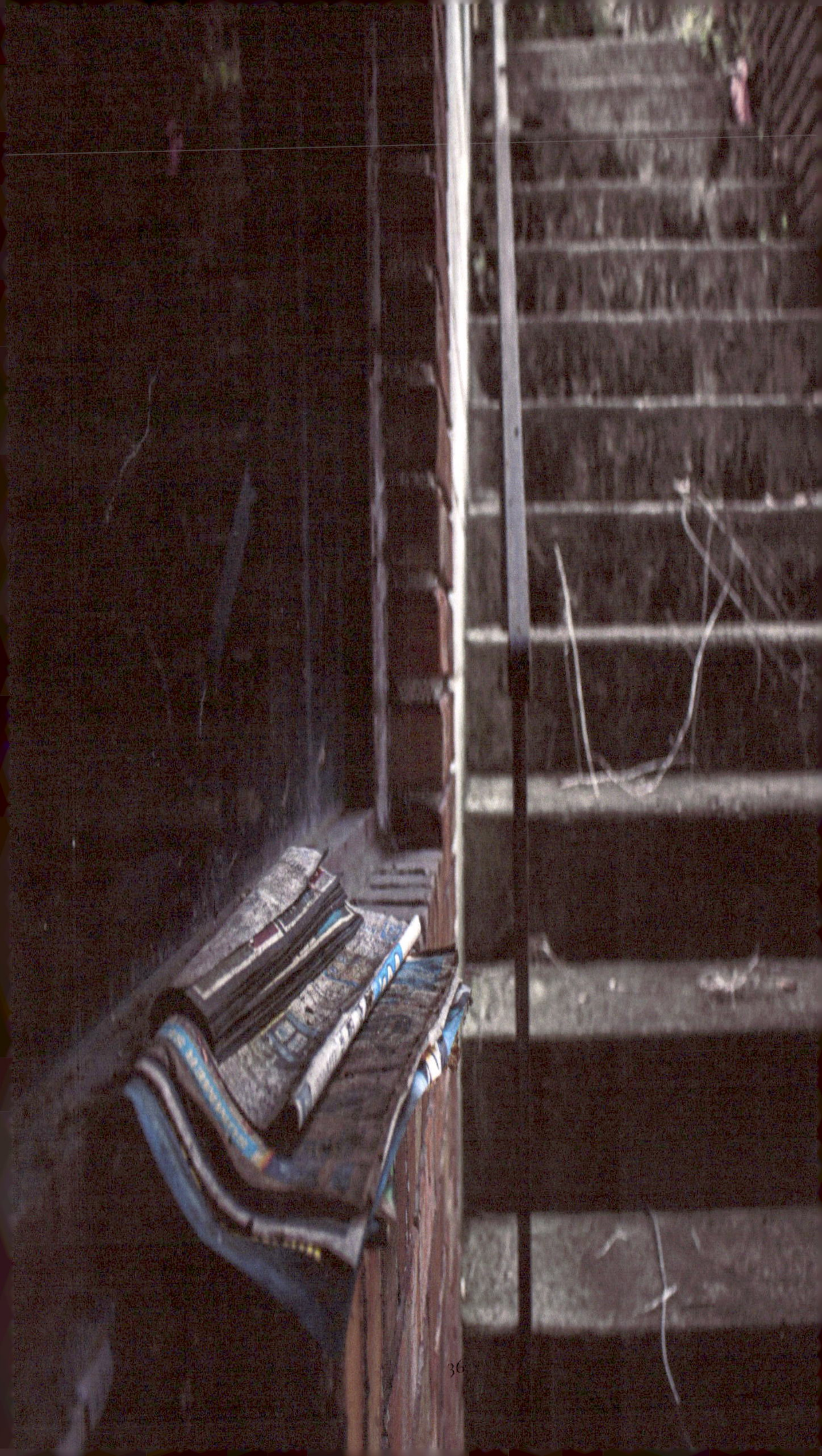
36

SOME TIME AGO;

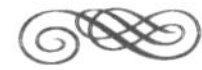

There is a certain sound to being lost;
And it changes with every set of eyes.
To some it looks like cherry blossoms
At night, illuminated by a lit cigarette.
To others it tastes of menthol and alcohol,
Still others see it in the reflection of rain
Gathered in puddles at their feet. I heard
It at the witching hour - in city streets left
Only with silence and the ghosts of sleep.

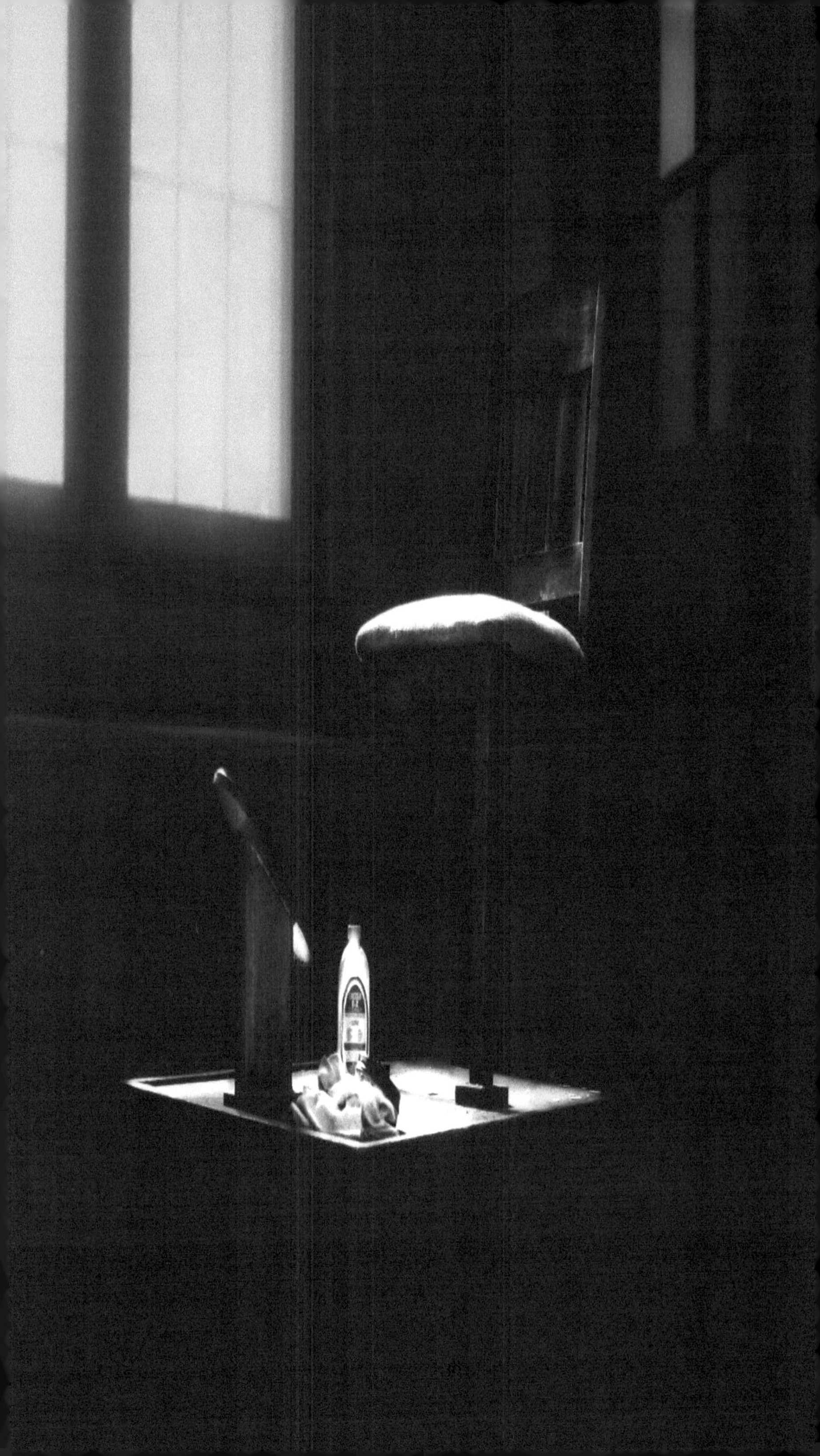

THE STARLIT GHOSTS

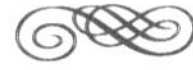

Gentle is forgotten light,
Cascading down to delight
The ghosts it mirrors.
Such a simple story;
Bygone worries dance adorned
With dust & old memories.
And so luminescent shadows
Pirouette all around - singing
Of starlight on the ground.

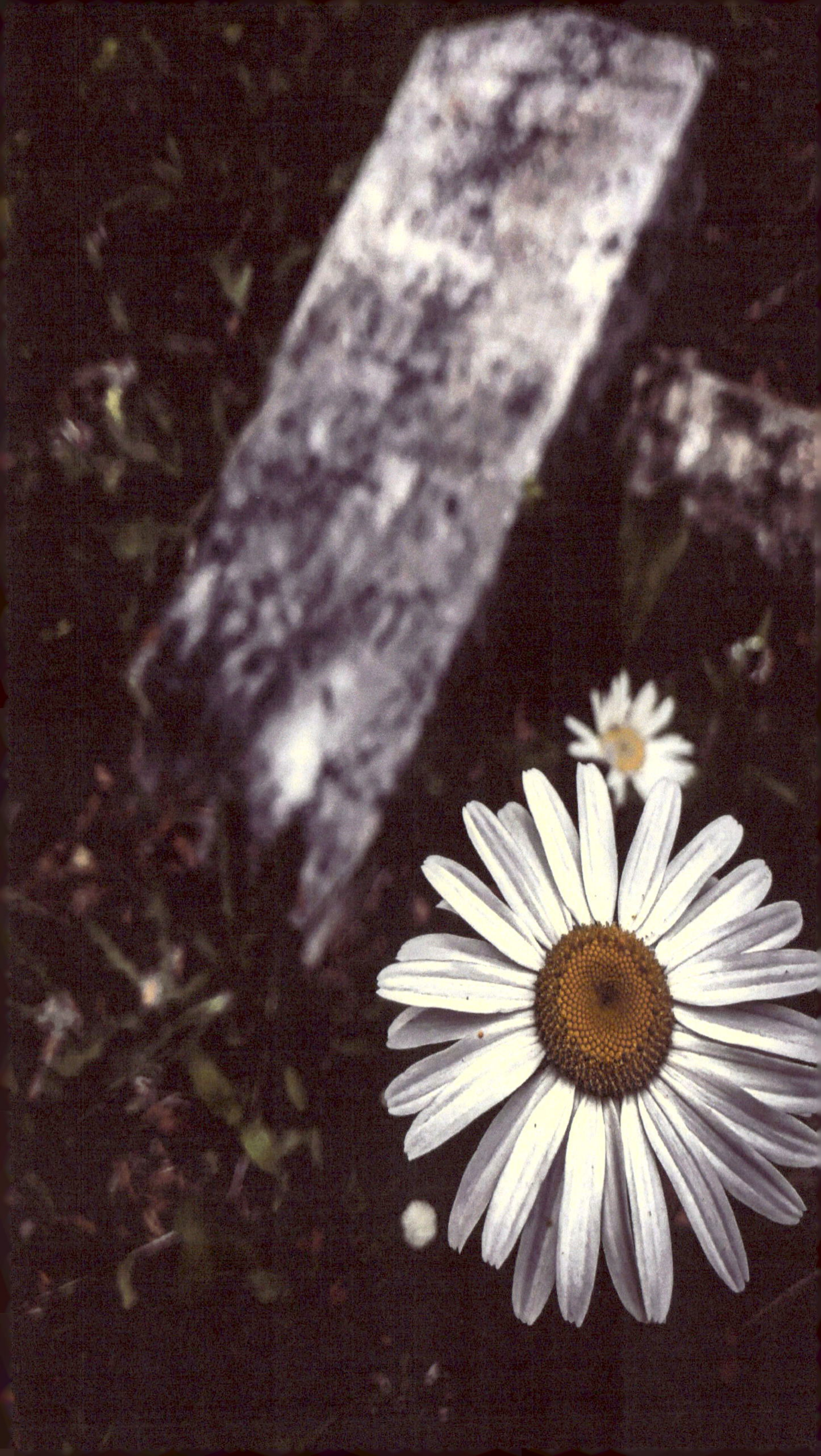

TOMBSTONE PETALS

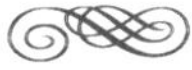

Flowers grow from the graves
Of silent ones slumbering below;
Their stories snake from withered bones
With the eons of knowledge they know.
Until, one day, fingers pick their whispers
And paragraphs like petals fall just so -
Their iridescent colors scatter to collect
In a pool of wisdom just below.

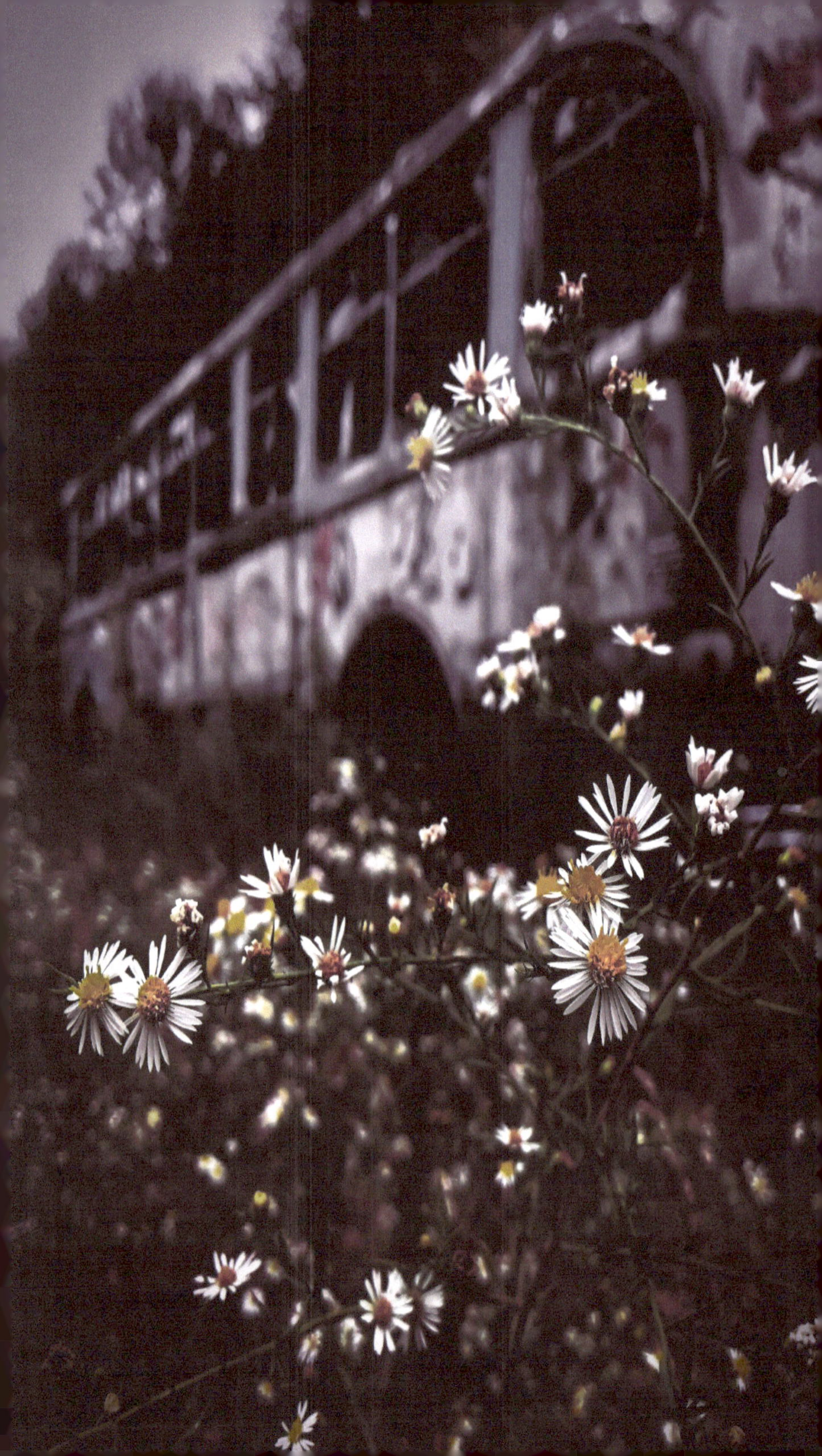

COLLATERAL PETAL

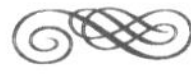

I'm writing this for you,
Flower thief. It's funny,
I told myself I'd never
Let it happen again, but I
Can only assume that I'm
The petal that falls once
You've clipped the stem.
Not to worry, my friend.
The breeze is quite beautiful
At such a day's quiet end.

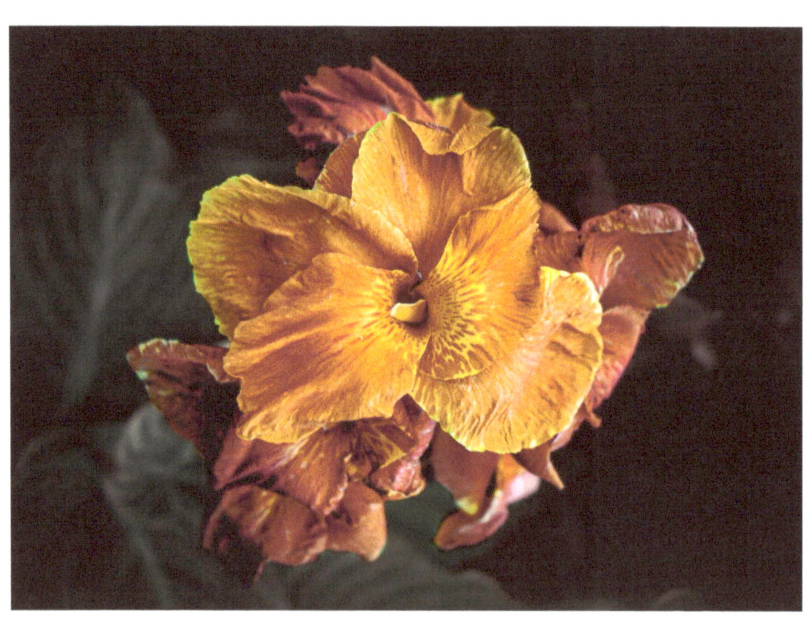

WILD CHILD

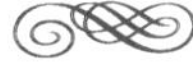

Make no mistake - she was not
Perfectly kept and tended to by
Loving hands each night and day,
As such a fragile thing aught.
She was wild - she was free;
She lived amongst the broken
Things, took root in a crack of
Pavement and bloomed her
Vibrant petals for all to see.

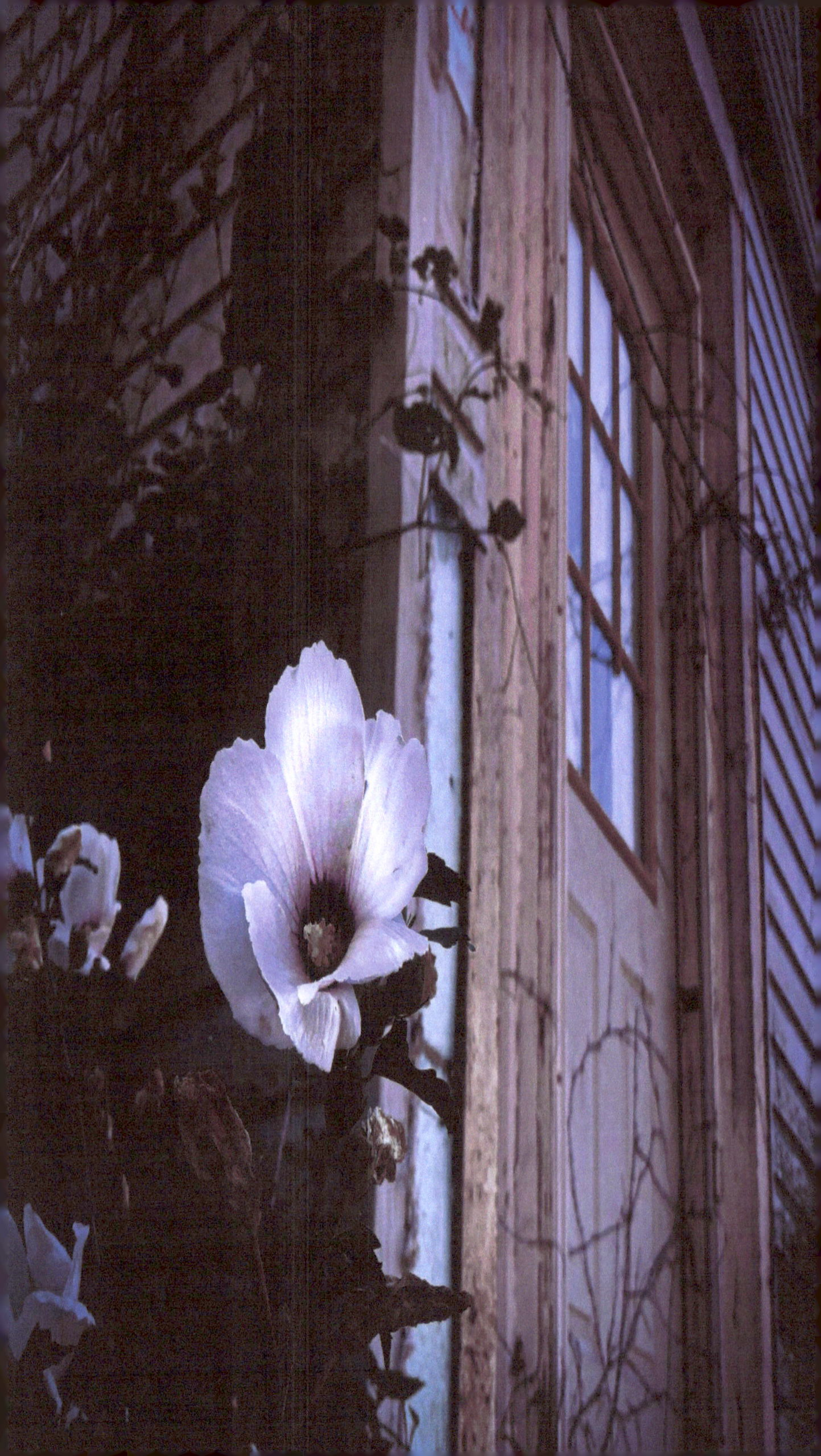

MOONLIGHT'S VOICE

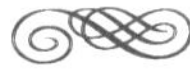

"It is natural," they told their babes,
  "For the moon to shine with light
Reflected from the sun." So innocent
Eyes dimmed, a dampness set within
Young minds - deeply, a seed was sown.
Quietly, she has waited. Patiently, she
Contemplated this contempt of man -
For she never wished to shine at all.
"What gall!" They decried; as though
This apathy stole essence from their sun.
"Yes, what a pity," her daughters replied.
For how much has been lost to fragile
Ego and narcissistic, masculine minds?
So much mystery admitted as insanity,
  Femininity lost to time.

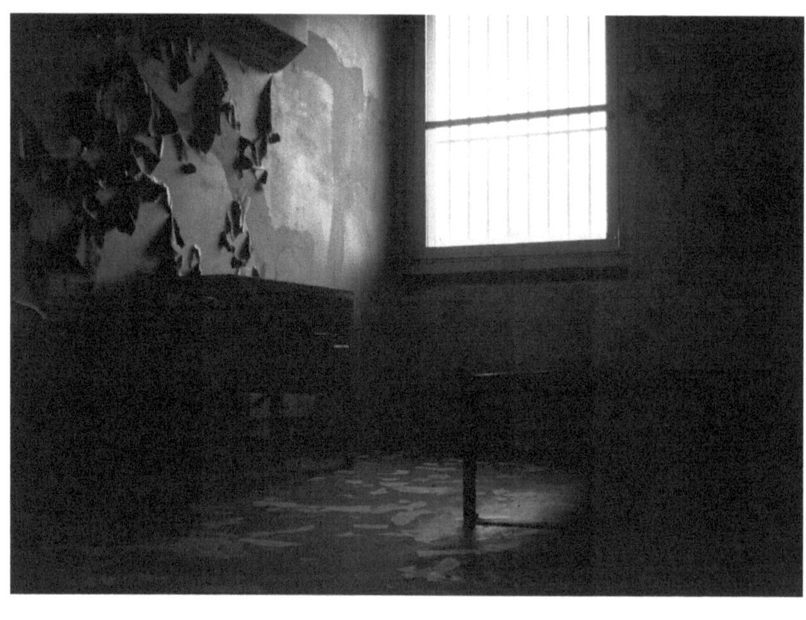

FOR MOONLIGHT;

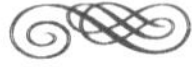

A delicate sort of dark -
The moonlight caresses
Sleeping foliage as it dreams
Of whispered words forgotten
In the dead of night.
So subtle is this light,
But beautiful nevertheless.
How clever it is in its love
Of luminescent quietness.

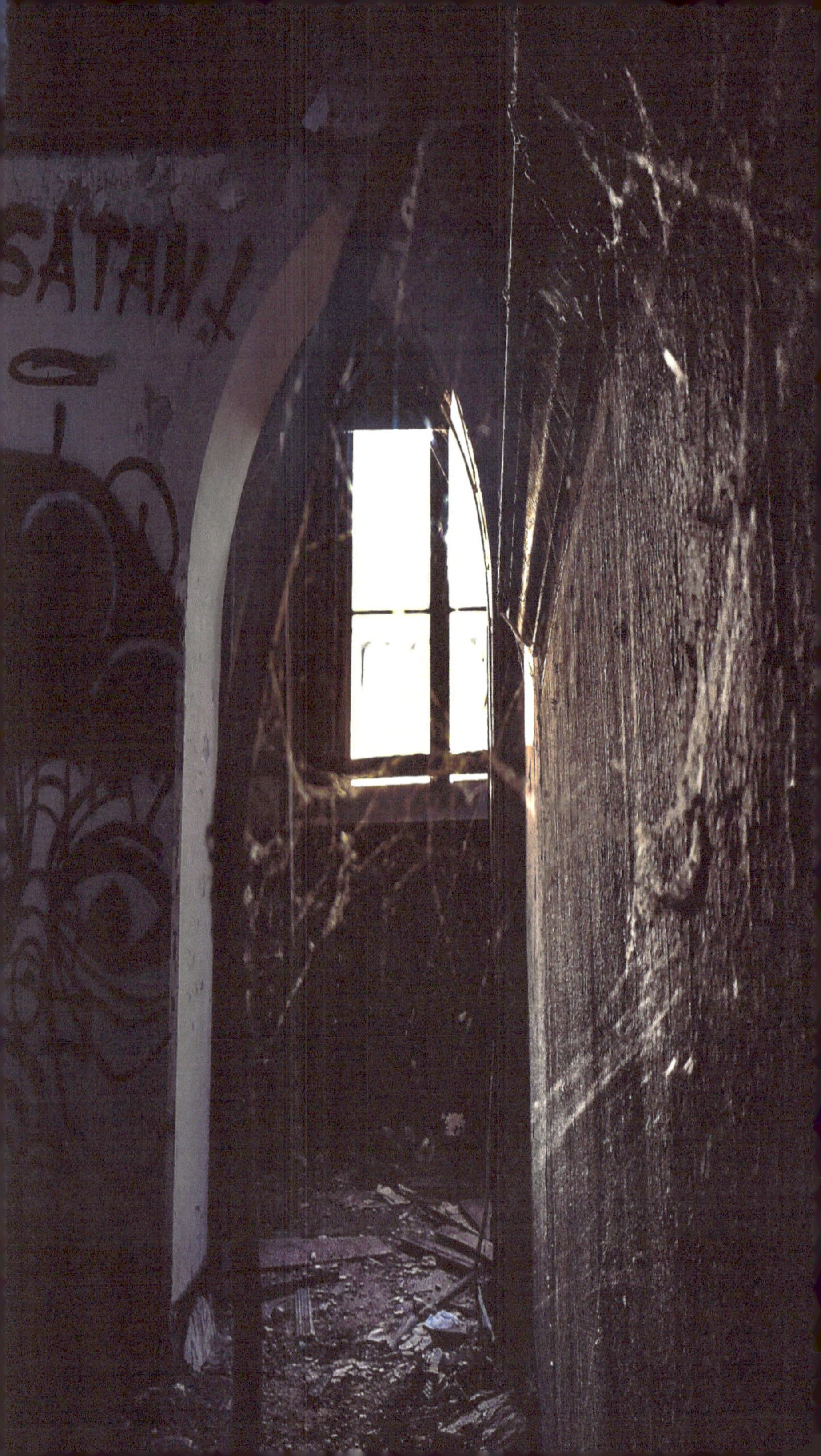
SATAN

THE WEB

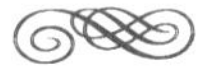

A spider weaves a web of Fate;
We waltz among its threads.
The morning dew collects and spreads
The clever colors it creates.
"Cease this fear of what will be,"
She laughs,
"What is to come will come."
For as we live and die in turn,
Eternal we become.

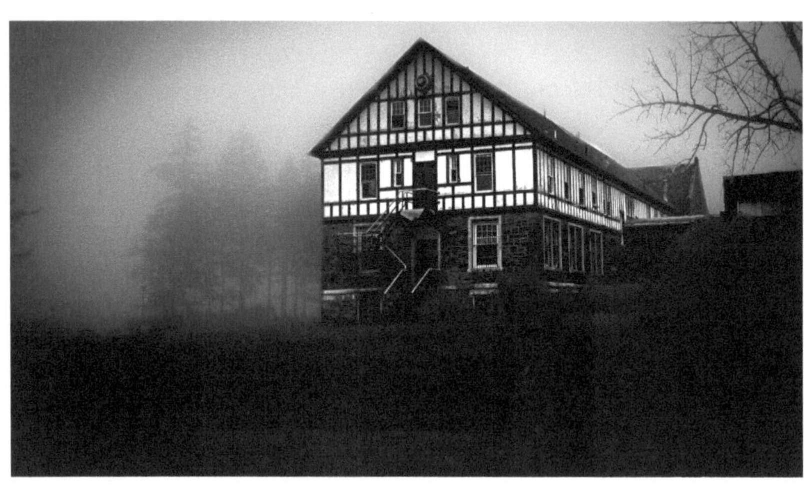

FACES IN THE FOG

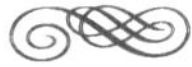

I think the clouds see ghosts, and
Perhaps even walk among them.
Both grace the ground without a sound,
Their secrets safe in silence - though
Whispers of memory are always in reverie.
And so the story goes, listen closely
For as those voices say -
"The world's a dream, nightmare or not,
So choose what ending it will play."

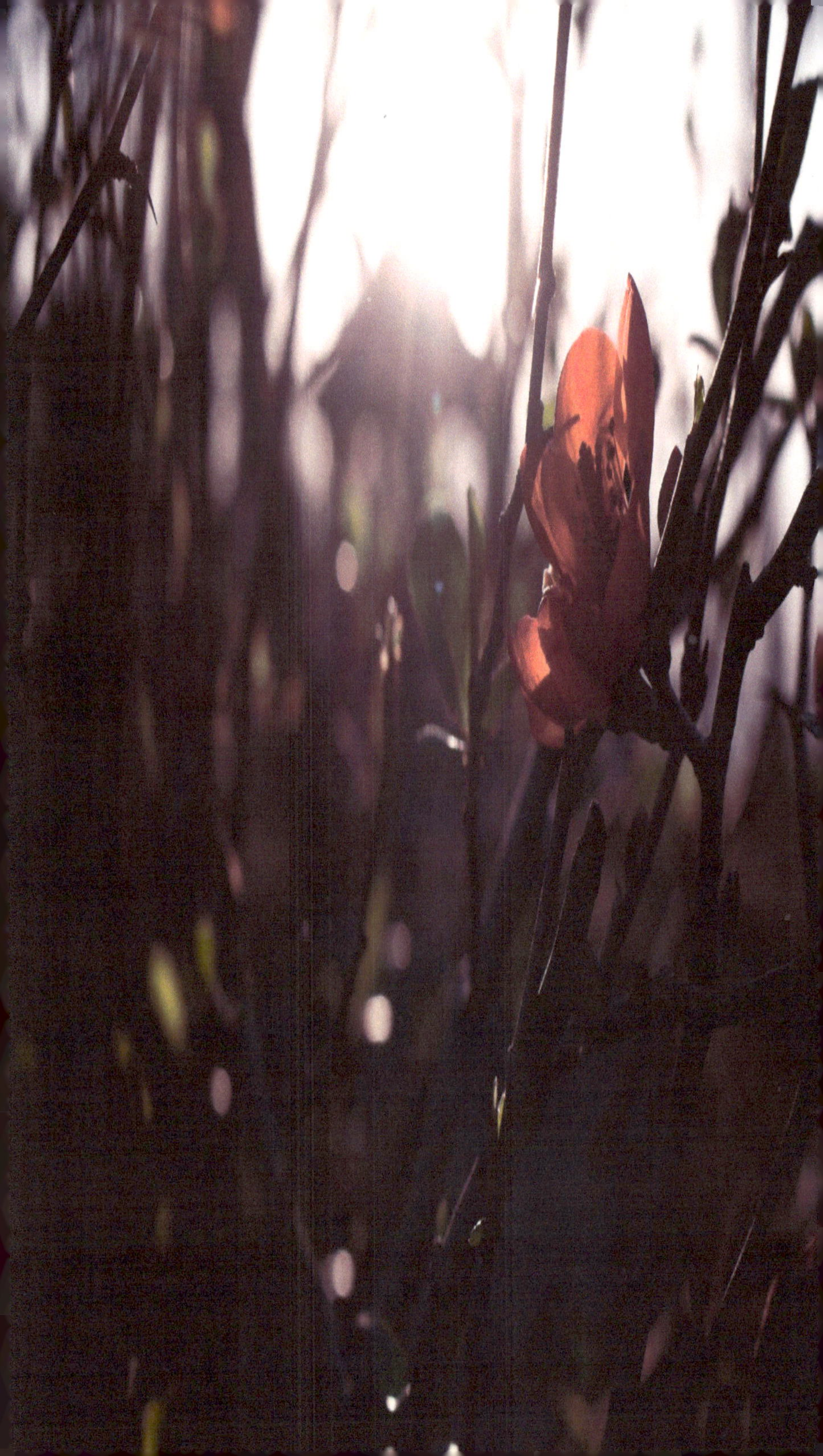

BLISSFUL BROKENNESS

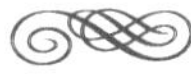

The answer flows like water -
Takes whatever shape it needs,
And from it grows a simple adage
Imperative for us to heed;
Some will learn to swim - still
Others condemned to drown - for
Soon these fragile, mortal shells
Coalesce with flowers in the ground.

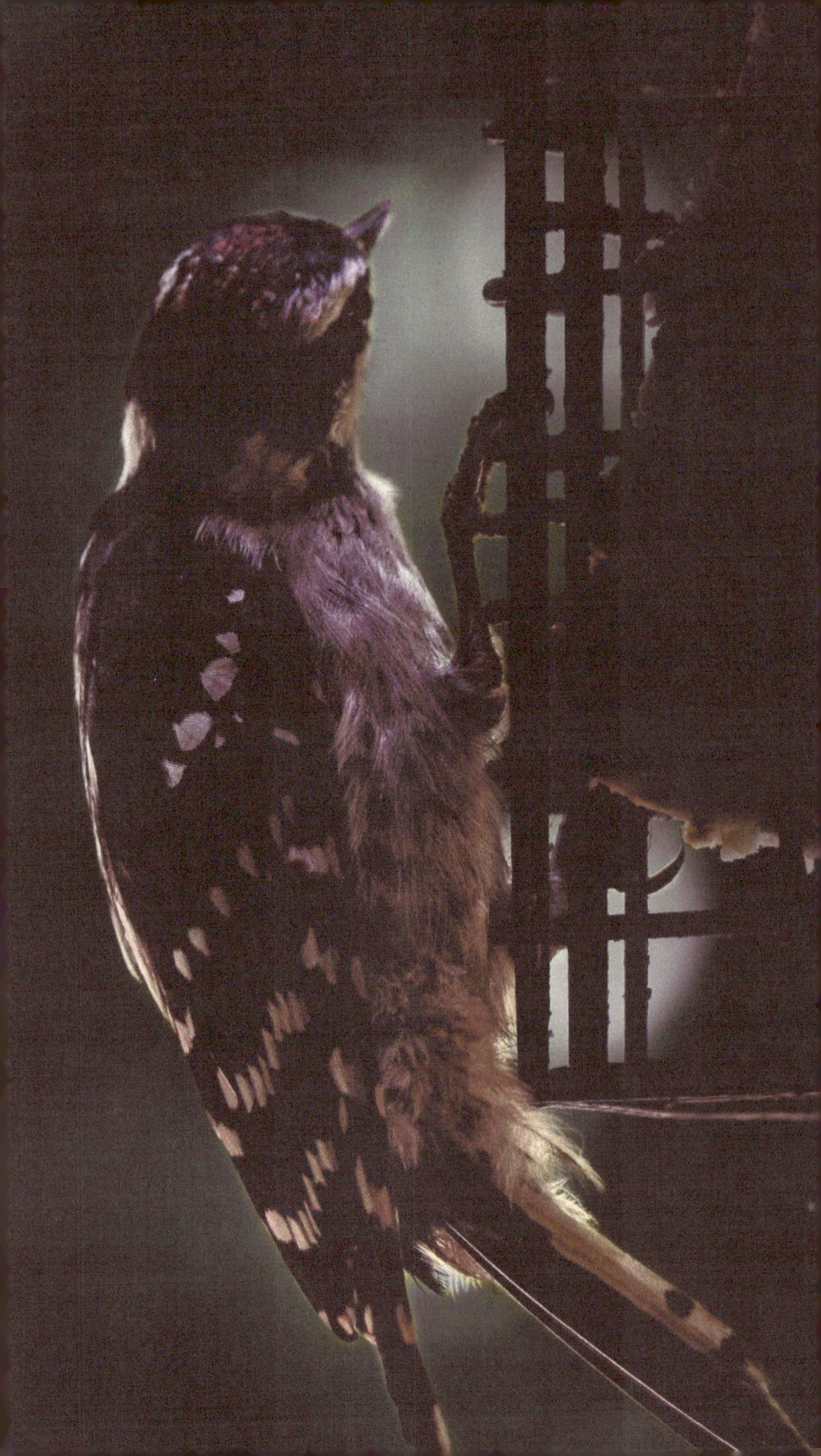

BLACKBIRD

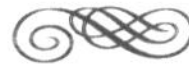

How free is the blackbird's song -
Both lovely & lonely alike, though
These solitary moments breathe
Incandescent silence into life.
And so this story goes, feathers
Of ink lost above the ground -
In love with flight and a calm
Within the chaos that's been found.

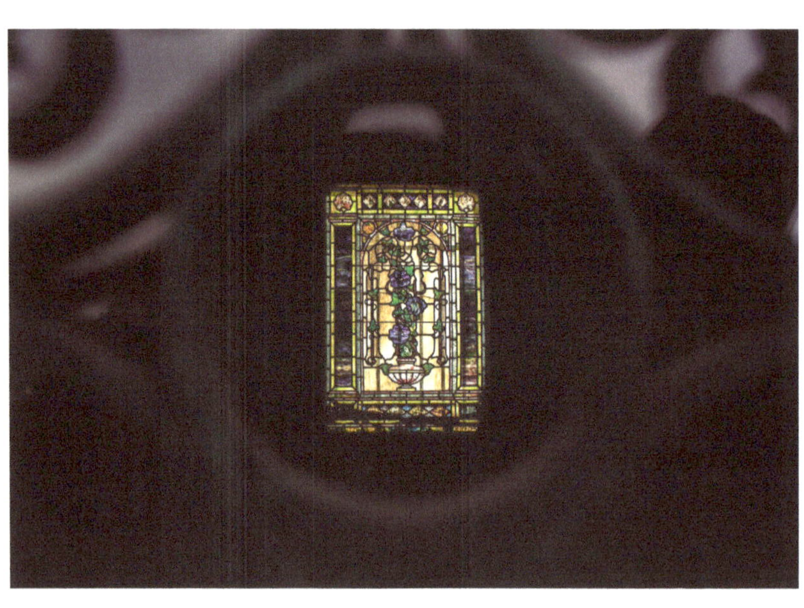

LIMINAL

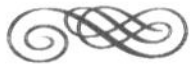

Do you see the world beyond the window?
The mysteries we seek framed by
Stones etched with fossils - engraved
With the echo of lives passed. Memories
Cast shadows in the graves, and if
You listen closely you'll hear the essence ask -
"What is it that awaits behind the glass?"

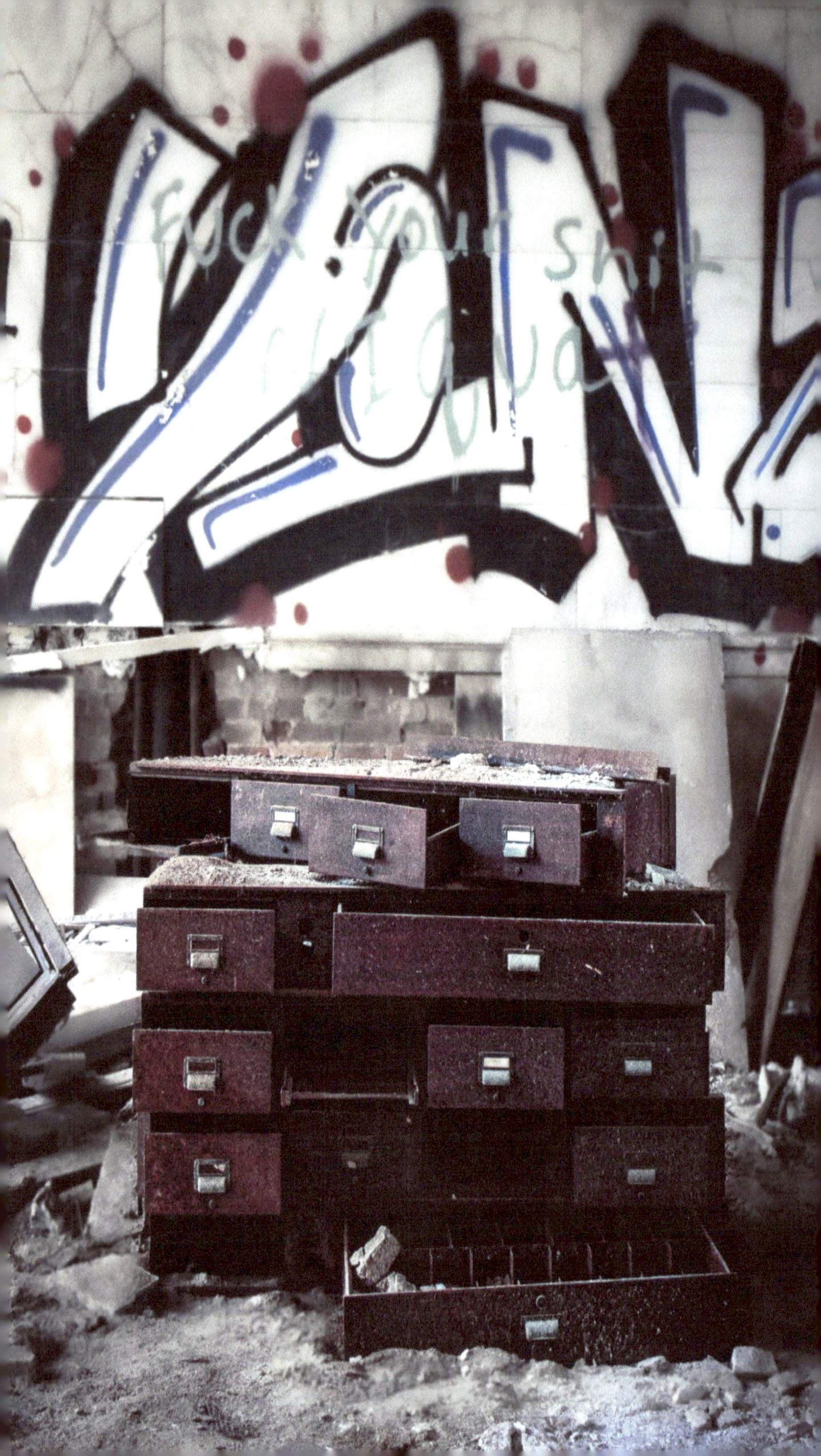
Fuck your shit

SECONDHAND

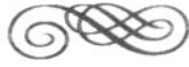

We wear time like the finest of silks;
She lines our bodies in wrinkles and
Folds. Fashions fade over the years,
But beauty has always been in the
Stories she tells - sketched on the
Canvas of our skin.

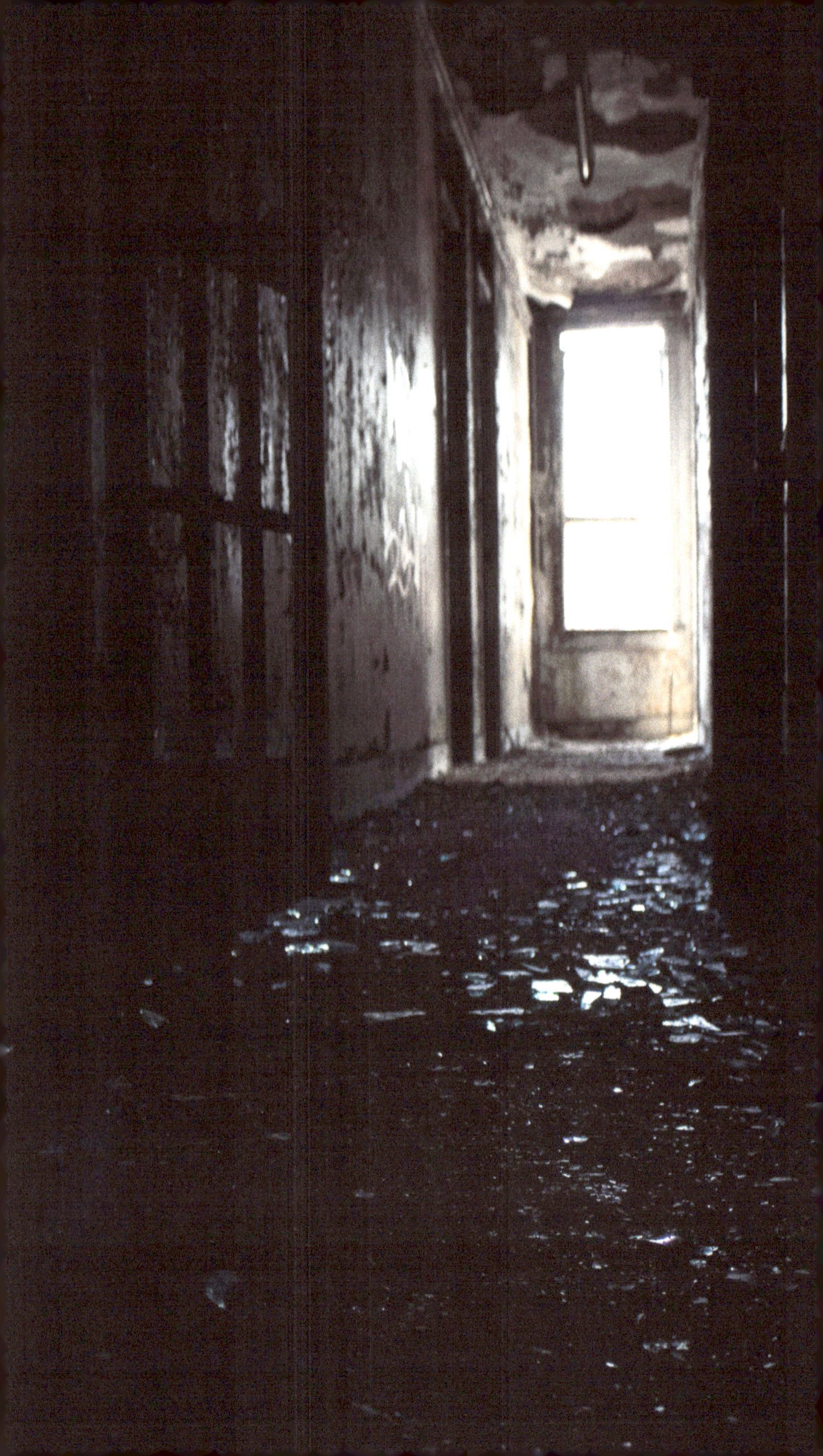

DANCE

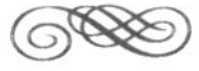

I walk down life's corridors,
Past empty rooms and chipping paint;
Time sings his song and from it falls
Leaves of once-color, now naught but
Pieces that crunch beneath my feet.
There is music in each creak -
Can you hear it? For there is something
In its stead, quiet under each beat;
Where once was, there is now - when the note
Strips naked to its core and takes a breath -
In it I hear Life and Death.

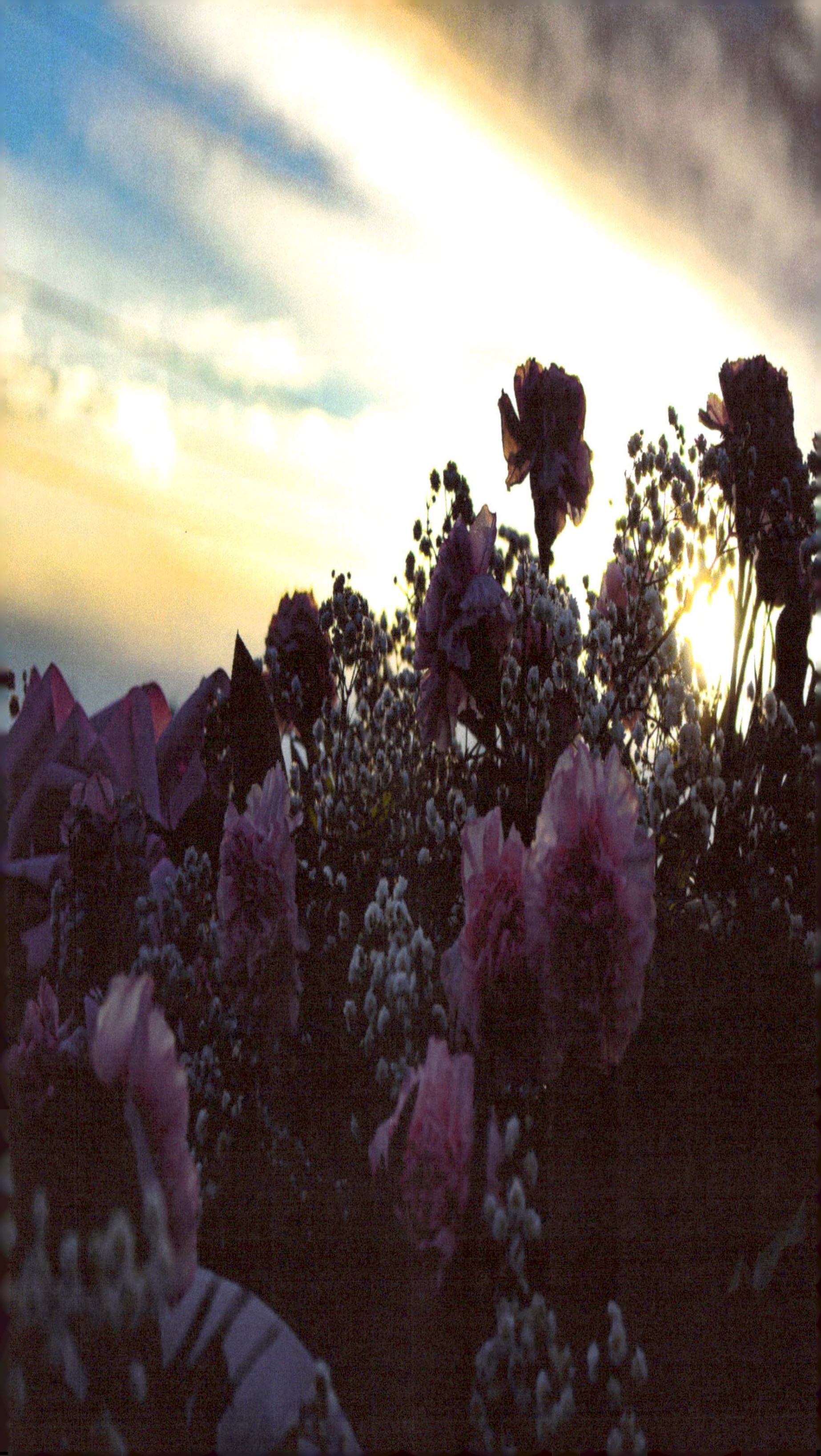

EULOGY

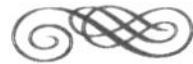

When I am laid to rest,
Burn me like the passion
I held in my chest is now
Nothing but ash and dust;
Scatter me among the wild
Flowers and ocean breeze -
Remember me when petals
Fall and wind rustles
Between the leaves.

EPILOGUE

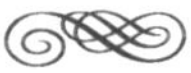

The Gremlin's Poem,
by Binx

epl;.-=============================lo
[sa;”””””””””””””” f5 588””’no9i98
Dms
Cvi[;””pQ8 97oOP5

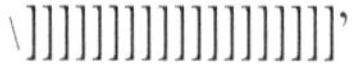

Acknowledgements

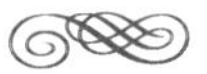

I'd like to start off by thanking my mom for passing on her love of words to me. I can only hope that one day she publishes her novel, too. I'd also like to thank everyone over the years who've allowed me to share my poetry with them. Whether we're still friends now, or have since grown apart, it means the world to me. A special thanks to the love of my life, Ryan, for pushing me to finally compile all of these poems into a book, and for believing in me no matter what. Most importantly though, I'd like to thank you, the reader. The thought of you supporting me by purchasing, and reading, these words, is something I'd never thought would happen in my wildest dreams. Even if only a handful of you do, and this book falls into the depths of obscurity - it means more than you know that you've made it this far and you're still here reading. I appreciate you, more than you could ever know.